Lady Margaret Pole: Countess of Salisbury

A Tudor Times Insight

By Tudor Times

Published by Tudor Times Ltd

Tudor Times Insights

Tudor Times Insights are books collating articles from our website www.tudortimes.co.uk which is a repository for a wide variety of information about the Tudor and Stewart period 1485 – 1625. There you can find material on People, Places, Daily Life, Military & Warfare, Politics & Economics and Religion. The site has a Book Review section, with author interviews and a book club. It also features comprehensive family trees, and a 'What's On' event list with information about forthcoming activities relevant to the Tudors and Stewarts.

Titles in the Series

Contents

Lady Margaret Pole: Countess of Salisbury

Introduction

In the Middle Ages, the Wheel of Fortune was a popular motif, showing the transience of everything – no matter how high you might be today, soon, the Wheel would turn and you too would be brought low, whilst another took your place. The history of Margaret, Countess of Salisbury can be seen as a perfect example of this mediaeval narrative, as her life moved from wealth and magnificence, to poverty and obscurity, then back to power and influence, before descending into a pit of dishonour and death.

Part 3 contains Lady Margaret Pole's Life Story and additional articles about her, looking at different aspects of her life. Margaret wielded power and influence more commonly in the hands of men, and this made her a political figure, in a way unusual for women of the sixteenth century. This position affected both the way she lived, and the reasons for her death.

Family Tree

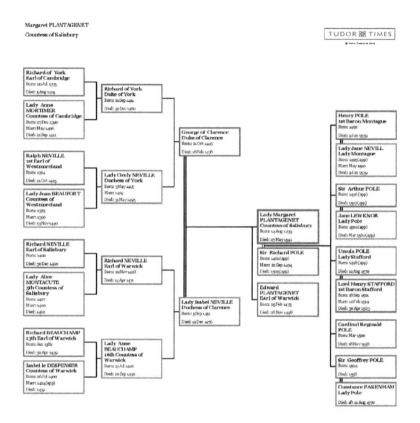

Lady Margaret Pole's Life Story

Chapter 1: Daughter of Clarence (1473 – 1487)

Margaret was born at the top of Fortune's Wheel, at the castle of Farleigh in Somerset. Her father, George, Duke of Clarence, was the brother of Edward IV, and her mother, Isabel Neville, was the daughter of that hero (or villain) of the Wars of the Roses, Warwick the Kingmaker. Isabel Neville, and her sister Anne, married to Clarence's brother, Richard, Duke of Gloucester, were co-heiresses to two of the greatest earldoms in England – Salisbury and Warwick, both of which were earldoms that could be inherited by women.

Clarence and Gloucester had quarrelled bitterly over the division of the spoils when Warwick the Kingmaker had been killed at Barnet. His widow, Anne, who was Countess of Warwick in her own right, was despoiled by her sons-in-law and treated as though she were naturally dead with the brothers sharing out her lands which covered great swathes of the south-west, the midlands and the north of England.

The household into which Margaret was born was the apogee of mediaeval power, wealth and 'good lordship', as the ties binding great peers to their supporters was known. The Clarence household was waited on by some 350 servants of all ranks, as they divided their time between Farleigh Castle, the mighty Warwick Castle, and their other numerous estates, transported by their 133 horses.

For the first eighteen months of Margaret's life, she was the Clarences' only child, until, in 1475, Duchess Isabel gave birth to a son, Edward. But Fortune's Wheel was turning and Isabel died in a third childbed, a year later, and was buried at the great Benedictine Abbey of Tewkesbury, which had been patronised by her Despenser and Beauchamp ancestors. Young Edward was confirmed by his uncle, the King, as Earl of Warwick, but the Salisbury inheritance, confiscated from Warwick the Kingmaker, remained vested in the Crown.

Soon after the loss of her mother, Margaret's father, a foolish, indiscreet, impulsive and injudicious man, for all his charm and good looks, fell foul, not for the first time, of his brother, Edward IV. Among his various misdeeds had been an alliance with Lancaster, in the years before Margaret's birth, and an attempt to upstage Edward IV by seeking to marry the great heiress, Mary, Duchess of Burgundy, against his brother's strict commands. Clarence receive a show-trial in Parliament, where the only accuser and prosecutor was the King himself, and the only defender was Clarence in person, no others being allowed to speak. Parliament found him guilty and he was executed in the Tower of London. According to legend, he was dispatched by being drowned in a butt of malmsey wine.

Clarence was not only condemned to death, he was also 'attainted' which meant his lands, goods and titles were forfeit to the Crown. As Margaret's brother had already been confirmed as Earl of Warwick, his father's death did not affect his status, but she had no inheritance, and was dependent entirely on King Edward for her maintenance. Edward took his duty seriously, and Margaret, referred to in the accounts as his 'dear and well-beloved niece', was clothed, educated and served at his expense, although her precise whereabouts during the remainder of Edward IV's reign are unknown.

It seems probable that she was brought into the household of the queen, Elizabeth Woodville, and her cousins, the King's children, who varied in age between Elizabeth, seven years older than Margaret, and

Bridget, seven years younger. Margaret's education would have been typical of that of a member of the royal family – reading, writing, keeping accounts, music (she played the virginals) sewing, both plain and fine, and, probably, French.

In 1483, political events changed Margaret's life again. Edward IV died, but his young son, proclaimed Edward V, never saw his coronation, his place being taken by his uncle Gloucester, now crowned as Richard III. As Clarence had been the older brother of the two, there were grounds for suggesting that Warwick was the legitimate heir if there were problem with the inheritance of Edward IV's children, but that idea was not likely to take root.

Again, Margaret's exact location during the next two years is uncertain, but by the time of the Battle of Bosworth in August 1485, when Richard III was defeated by Henry Tudor, Earl of Richmond, Margaret, her brother, and her female cousins, were all at the impressive Castle of Sheriff Hutton in Yorkshire. The new king, Henry VII, had vowed to marry Elizabeth of York should he be victorious, and the York princesses and Margaret were placed in the household of his mother, Lady Margaret Beaufort, Countess of Richmond and Derby. Initially, Warwick was there, too.

Lady Margaret Beaufort was a clever, intelligent and well-connected woman, devoted to her son's interests, and, although Henry VII was not a man to rely on anyone, he was close to his mother, and trusted her completely. By placing the Yorkist heirs in her care, he could be sure that they would be both safe, and kept away from anyone plotting on their behalf. In February 1486, Henry married Elizabeth, and Margaret became an important member of their court. She was listed, under the title '*My Lady Margaret of Clarence*', as the first of the great ladies attending the baptism of the royal heir, Arthur, in September of 1486. Fortune's Wheel was beginning to turn again in Margaret's favour.

Edward, Earl of Warwick, however, was not so fortunate as his sister. In 1487, whispers of a rebellion were abroad, with a young man, Lambert Simnel, claiming to be him. Warwick, no more than eleven years old, was paraded through the streets of London, to prove that Simnel was an imposter, then incarcerated in the Tower. Simnel's backers, Margaret's paternal aunt, Margaret, Duchess of Burgundy and her cousin, John de la Pole, Earl of Lincoln, raised an army greater than that brought by Henry VII to Bosworth, but were heavily defeated at the Battle of Stoke in November 1487.

Immediately following the battle, Elizabeth of York was crowned, reminding everyone of her status as the senior York heir. Margaret was present, watching the ceremony from a private viewing stage she shared with the King and Lady Margaret Beaufort. Margaret remained at court, but Warwick's estates were confiscated on 30 November 1487. Eventually, in 1490, the lands were returned to Margaret and Edward's grandmother, Anne, Countess of Warwick, who had been defrauded by her sons-in-law, twenty years before. Countess Anne was obliged to disinherit her grandson and leave her lands to the King. Edward, still referred to as Earl of Warwick, retained some of the Salisbury lands, for the time being, at least, although they were little use to him in the Tower.

Chapter 2: Tudor Matron (1487 – 1504)

In the aftermath of the Battle of Stoke, Henry VII was keener than ever to prevent any risk of Yorkist heirs popping up. His sister-in-law, Cicely of York, was married to the Tudor stalwart John, Viscount Welles, Henry's half-uncle, and Margaret was given in marriage to Sir Richard Pole. The marriage date of Margaret and Richard is usually given as

1491, but her biographer, Hazel Pierce, has made an excellent case for it being 1487, as a result of the Simnel rebellion.

It was later suggested that Margaret was '*disparaged*' by the marriage – that is, her royal blood was sullied by a match to such a low-born man, however, that is not entirely fair. Sir Richard, knighted after the Battle of Stoke, was Henry VII's half-cousin, and though not of royal blood, he was much favoured by the King and given many honourable positions.

Sir Richard was around fifteen or sixteen years older than Margaret. His father, Geoffrey, had been a trusted councillor of Jasper Tudor, Earl of Pembroke, and his mother, Edith St John, was Margaret Beaufort's much-cherished half-sister. Nevertheless, Margaret, whose father's income had been £6,000 per annum, might have been a little disgruntled at a husband whose landed wealth amounted to no more than £50. Margaret had no dowry, however, so this was a slight improvement over dependence on Henry and Elizabeth. In order to maintain his royally-connected bride, Sir Richard was given two more manors, bringing his income up to the pleasant, but hardly princely, sum of £170 per annum, supplemented by the income from his various offices.

Initially, Margaret lived on her husband's manor of Bockmer, Buckinghamshire, but was still present at court from time to time, in attendance on both Queen Elizabeth and Lady Margaret Beaufort at the Feast of St George in April 1488, and at Christmas that year. Her name appeared after the Queen's sisters and the other peeresses. In 1493, Margaret received the uncharacteristically generous present of £20 from Henry VII, perhaps as an adjunct to Richard's appointment to the prestigious office of Chamberlain to Arthur, Prince of Wales.

It is likely (although the exact timings are disputed) that it was at this time that Arthur's independent household was set up at Ludlow. Margaret and Richard moved to Staffordshire, being granted the use of Stourton Castle, near Kinver. Richard had a number of offices in Wales, in addition to the position as Chamberlain: Sheriff of Merioneth, Constable of Harlech Castle and later Constable of North Wales, and Constable of Chester, and this location would enable him to be on hand to perform his duties.

Throughout the 1490s Richard was busy on royal business, travelling around the kingdom, and taking part in Henry VII's few foreign forays to Brittany and France. He was also honoured in 1499 by being appointed as a Knight of the Garter. Membership of the Order of the Garter was a most prestigious accolade, and Richard, a few years later, was noted as 'rychly arayed in his Coller' at the proxy wedding of Henry VII's daughter (yet another Margaret) to James IV of Scotland.

Margaret's first son had been born in 1492, and named, not surprisingly, Henry. Her next three children, Arthur, Reginald and Ursula, were born at intervals up to 1500 and her last son, Geoffrey in 1504. There may have been another daughter who died young.

These tranquil years, spent between the Welsh Marches, the Court and the Pole manor at Bockmer were rudely interrupted in 1499 when, as a result of the long-drawn out Perkin Warbeck affair, her brother, Warwick, was executed.

The treatment of Warwick is a dark stain on Henry VII's reign, and something he apparently felt guilty about later. The Earl, confined to the Tower since 1486, had not been properly educated or attended, and it is almost certain that the attempted escape with Warbeck, for which he was charged with treason, was a put-up job. Henry VII at least had the grace to have Warwick properly interred at Bisham Priory, resting place of the Earls of Salisbury, and paid for the funeral.

Another person who claimed later to feel guilt over Warwick's death was Katharine of Aragon, whose parents, Ferdinand and Isabella, had insinuated that the marriage between Katharine and Prince Arthur could not take place whilst there was the least risk to Henry's throne.

There is no record of Margaret's reaction, but it seems reasonable to suppose that she was deeply upset by the loss of her brother in such tragic circumstances. Her later petition to Henry VIII for the restoration of the Earldom of Salisbury proclaims her belief that, if he had been drawn into treason, it was through innocence and ignorance. Warwick's attainder for treason meant that his inheritance was confiscated, so Margaret, although she was his heir, received nothing.

Whatever her inner feelings, Margaret had her duty to perform, and soon she would have a more pleasing one. Prince Arthur was married to the Spanish Princess in 1501, and the young couple took up residence at Ludlow, with Margaret almost certainly amongst the English ladies appointed to attend the Princess, whilst her husband continued in his role as Prince Arthur's Lord Chamberlain.

Whether Katharine favoured Margaret initially because of the circumstances of Warwick's death, or whether it was genuine regard, the two women struck up a close friendship, despite Margaret being some twelve years the elder.

Shockingly, within five months of his marriage, Arthur was dead, and the royal household broken up. Katharine returned to London, and Margaret and Richard continued to divide their time between Stourton and Bockmer.

But Fortune's Wheel turned again - in October 1504, either just before, or just after Margaret bore her last child, Geoffrey, Sir Richard Pole died, and Margaret was left a widow of small means and dangerous royal blood.

Chapter 3: Widows & Orphans (1504 – 1509)

Sir Richard's salary for the various offices he held would have ceased upon his death, and Margaret's dower rights would have been no more than her common-law entitlement of one-third of the £170 landed income from his manors in Buckinghamshire – as she had brought no dowry to the marriage, she is unlikely to have had a more generous jointure. The lands themselves were held by the King, as was customary, during the minority of the heir, Margaret's eldest son, Henry.

There was no family to whom Margaret could turn – her cousin, Elizabeth of York, who had frequently made presents of money to her sisters when they were in straitened circumstances, had died in 1503. The other York princesses, if they had any ready cash (Cicely had been banished and her lands confiscated in 1503 for making a disgraceful marriage and Bridget was a nun) may not have wished to draw attention to themselves by supporting Warwick's sister.

Margaret did receive some support from Richard's friend, Charles Somerset, a distant cousin of the King, who stood surety with her for a loan of £40 for the funeral, and two rather grudging bits of support from King Henry, who permitted the funeral loan to be repaid out of the income from the Pole lands and gave her just over £55 for food and clothes.

It does not seem a huge amount, given the years of loyalty Sir Richard had shown Henry, and the fact that the King was sitting on the vast Salisbury and Warwick estates that were Margaret's hereditary portion. Margaret and her children remained in the country, with her third son, Reginald, being sent to the Carthusian Monastery at Sheen when he was around seven, to be trained to the scholarly life.

Meanwhile, Margaret's friend, Katharine of Aragon, dowager Princess of Wales, was also hard up, and dependent on the unenthusiastic charity of her father-in-law. This joint experience of widowhood and poverty proved another link between the two women. But, just as things seemed at their lowest ebb, the Wheel of Fortune turned again, and Margaret moved into the limelight.

Chapter 4: Countess of Salisbury (1509 – 1521)

Henry VII died in 1509, and within weeks, Margaret had been whisked to court as the Lady-in-Waiting of the new Queen, Katharine of Aragon. Forty marks were shelled out by the new King for Margaret's board after her arrival in London for the coronation. Henry VIII, who may have remembered Margaret from his early childhood, showed himself willing, initially, to favour the remaining members of his mother's family of York, and was also pleased to accede to any requests Katharine made for her friends to be promoted. Margaret's son, Henry, now 17, was immediately given a place in the King's household.

Margaret was still only the widow of a knight, but, for the coronation, she received the cloth allowance given to countesses – perhaps an early indication that the royal couple were contemplating the restoration of her family. She also received an annuity of £100.

Over the next couple of years, more marks of favour were granted – Henry Pole was promoted in the King's household and given fine clothes, and Reginald's education was paid for by the King.

During these early years of Henry VIII's reign, Margaret remained close to Queen Katharine, no doubt comforting the Queen after her 1510 miscarriage, and again after the devastating loss of Henry, Duke of Cornwall in 1511. In 1512, Margaret finally returned to the top of

Fortune's Wheel: her petition for restoration to the Earldom of Salisbury (see Margaret's family tree for her descent) was granted.

Salisbury was one of the oldest earldoms in the kingdom, and heritable by women – Margaret's great-grandmother had been Countess in her own right. Warwick was also heritable by women, but, for whatever reason, perhaps because it did not seem politic to ask too much, and because, legally, Henry VII had received the lands from Countess Anne by gift, rather than by confiscation, Margaret did not petition for that earldom to be restored.

Henry VIII's reasons for restoring the earldom were probably mixed – there was a general feeling that the execution of Warwick had been unjust and Henry wanted to contrast his generosity and open-handedness with Henry VII's niggardly later years. Katharine's support was probably helpful as well.

In the early years of his reign, with hopes of a male heir, Henry tried to weave the members of the wider royal family into a tight-knit unit, and promoted many of his Yorkist cousins, including restoring the son of his aunt, Katherine of York, to the Earldom of Devon, and later, promoting him to Marquess of Exeter. Not all Yorkist cousins were so fortunate – Edmund de la Pole (a different family from the Poles) was dragged out of the Tower and executed before Henry felt it safe to embark for France in 1512.

Of course, restoration of an earldom with an income of £2,000 per annum (some forty times the income Margaret had enjoyed as a widow) did not come free. Margaret paid the King 5,000 marks (c. £3,330 or eighteen months' income) as her entry fine. Margaret would not have had the cash to pay up front, so she must have borrowed the initial £1,000 she paid, and then she and her eldest son and heir, Henry, referred to thereafter as Henry, Baron Montague, were bound in a recognisance to pay the remainder.

Margaret, from being a poor widow, was now catapulted to the position of fifth or sixth richest noble in the land, after the King. It must have been a dizzying experience, and perhaps brought back traces of memory of her very early childhood.

Margaret, now Countess of Salisbury, took to her new-found wealth with delight, and recreated the lavish feudal household of her parents, with her arms plastered, painted, embroidered, and engraved on anything that stayed still long enough – clothes, tableware, window-glass, tapestries and horse-blankets. She had a London home, Le Herber (now under Cannon Street Station) as well as country seats at Clavering, Essex; Bisham, Buckinghamshire and Warblington in Hampshire, not forgetting the dozens of smaller manor houses she owned.

Despite such a choice of accommodation, Margaret continued her attendance at Court, and, in 1516 received the prestigious honour of standing as godmother at the Confirmation of the only child of Henry and Katharine to live more than a few weeks – Mary, born 18th February 1516.

It seems, too, that Henry and Katharine probably visited her at Warblington during their summer progresses and she received presents as generous, or more than as generous, at New Year, as the Dukes of Norfolk and Suffolk. The ultimate accolade of the King and Queen's affection and trust was her appointment as Lady Governess to Princess Mary in 1520.

Fortune could give no more, and inevitably, things began to go wrong.

Chapter 5: Suspicion (1521 – 1525)

Once Margaret had been restored to her inheritance, part of her duty was to arrange the best marriages she could afford for her children. In 1518 she arranged her son, Henry Pole's, marriage to Jane Neville, the daughter of Lord Bergavenny, and her daughter, Ursula's, marriage with the eldest son of Edward Stafford, 3rd Duke of Buckingham.

Buckingham was a descendant of Edward III, and the senior Duke in the kingdom. This was a splendid match for Ursula, who would, in due course, be the highest-ranking peeress in England, after the Queen, the Princess and the King's sisters. Margaret must have danced at the wedding with an exultant heart.

Unfortunately, Buckingham was not just a distant relative of the King, he had all the arrogance, pride in his royal blood and disdain for lesser ranks that had characterised his father, the Duke who had rebelled against Richard III, and also Margaret's own father, Clarence. Henry VIII was no more tolerant of over-mighty nobles than his great-uncle and grandfather had been and Buckingham had made the additional mistake of treating Henry VIII's chief minister, Cardinal Wolsey, with contempt.

In 1521, Buckingham was charged with treason. It does not appear that he was really involved in any plot to overthrow Henry VIII, but he had grumbled about upstarts, speculated on the succession (the King had no male heir, and Buckingham was a possible contender for the throne) and, prone to violent rages, talked wildly about killing the King. Regardless of the meat of the charge, Henry VIII believed there was a genuine threat to himself and the House of Tudor.

Buckingham and his servants were arrested and interrogated, and so was Henry Pole, Lord Montague. Montague was connected, both through being the brother-in-law of Buckingham's son, and the son-in-law of Buckingham's own son-in-law, Lord Bergavenny. Buckingham was executed on 17th May 1521 and a cloud of suspicion hung over the whole Pole family. Margaret was removed from her office of Lady Governess to the Princess.

After some months in the wilderness, the Poles began to come back into favour. Montague was released and chosen to attend the King at his meeting with Charles V in 1522, and Margaret again received New Year presents from the Queen. Ursula, of course, was now deprived of the prospect of becoming a Duchess, and never ranked higher than wife of Baron, with twelve children and a rather more limited income than expected.

Chapter 6: My Lady Governess (1525 – 1533)

By 1525, Margaret was reappointed to the role of Lady Governess to Princess Mary. By this point, it was clear that Mary would have no brothers, and Henry was obviously considering her as his heir, although he would never definitely commit to the idea. In 1525, Mary was sent to Ludlow in the Welsh Marches to hold Court as the de facto Princess of Wales, as her Uncle Arthur had been in 1501, and her great-uncle Edward V had in 1473. Mary was never officially invested with the title, but was referred to by it from time to time. Margaret went with her to supervise the household as she and Sir Richard Pole had done in 1501.

Margaret's duties were carefully documented. She had charge of the Princess' education (although the teaching was delivered by masters), her health, exercise, diet and recreation. Margaret, like the King and Queen, patronised the Humanist scholars of Oxford and Cambridge, but her religion was as orthodox as theirs, and she would have ensured that Mary continued to worship in the time-honoured Catholic fashion. There would have been little concession to the evangelical thought spreading its way across Europe and, with the emergence of Anne Boleyn as a rival to Katharine, into the Court.

During the period 1525-1528, Margaret and Mary were based in the Marches, but travelled in the region, and returned to London in 1527 for Mary's betrothal (her third, by the tender age of 11) to Henri, Duc d'Orleans, second son of François I of France. It was around this time that Margaret's son, Arthur, died.

By 1528, Katharine's position as Queen, and Mary's as Princess of Wales, was beginning to look decidedly precarious. Henry was attempting to have their marriage annulled, so that he could secure the succession with a male heir. Margaret was, presumably, deeply concerned for her friend and for her charge, but Mary's household, although reduced in size and recalled from Ludlow, continued much as before, with Margaret remaining in post.

Margaret and Mary spent the Christmases of 1529 and 1530 at Court, and Henry continued to treat his daughter with affection. Margaret's job must have become increasingly difficult – she would have wanted to shield Mary from the worst of the pain of the breakdown of her parents' marriage, but by the time Henry finally left Katharine in the summer of 1531, it would have been impossible for Mary, by then fifteen and a half, and so considered adult, not to know the full situation.

Until 1533, Margaret was not called upon actively to support Henry's actions against Katharine and the potential disinheriting of Mary, but in 1533, she was obliged to nail her colours to the mast when an order arrived from Thomas Cromwell to Mary's Lord Chamberlain, Lord Hussey. He was to hand over Mary's jewels, with an inventory, to a Mistress Frances Elmer. Margaret impeded the dispatch of the jewels so far as she could, delaying the production of an inventory, then slowly writing one herself which she ordered Hussey and the other household officials to sign. Still she delayed the handover, refusing to act until she received an order direct from the King.

Hussey excused his failure to obey orders by telling Cromwell that:

'In no wyse she (Margaret) wyll as yete deliyver to Mistress Frances the jewells for anything that I can say or doo onlesse that yt may please you to obteyne the kings letters unto hyr in that behalf.'

Follow up commands to Hussey from Cromwell to sell the Princess' silver plate were answered with the news that he couldn't do so, as the plate was in the hands of *'my lady Governesse.'* It was impossible, Margaret said, that the plate should be sold, as it was used frequently, and could not be disposed of unless replaced. Of course, Margaret added, if the King commanded directly, *'she will at all tymes be redy upon her discharge to make thereof delivery.'*

Henry was beset on all sides by stubborn women. Anne Boleyn was demanding Katharine of Aragon should hand over the christening robes used for her children, which tasteless request Katharine rejected indignantly; Mary was refusing to accept the validity of Henry's new marriage and the demotion from Princess of Wales, which occurred in September 1533; and Margaret was making heavy weather of carrying out any orders. One could almost pity the man.

Angry and frustrated, but still fond of his daughter, Henry reacted to Mary's disobedience by removing those about her, whom he could blame for her obstinacy. Margaret was dismissed from her post, and Mary was sent with only a few attendants to a humiliating position in the household of the recently born Elizabeth.

Margaret was clearly willing to take risks on Mary's behalf, and offered to serve her with a suitable household, at her own expense. Henry was taking no chances, and rejected the offer out of hand. The Imperial Ambassador, Eustace Chapuys, opined that Margaret had been removed to make it easier *'to cause (Mary) to die of grief or in some other way, or else compel her to renounce her rights'*. Mary, however, did not need Margaret's stiffening to remain resolved.

Chapter 7: Darkening Days (1533 – 1536)

Henry continued to harbour resentment of Margaret, and, in 1535, when Chapuys suggested she be re-appointed as Lady Governess, spoke of her contemptuously, saying *'the countess is a fool, of no experience.'* Margaret had annoyed Henry not only in relation to her support of Mary and Katharine, but also by ill-advisedly persisting in an argument over land rights.

Margaret's world was disintegrating – her dear friend, Katharine, had been banished to the draughty castle of Kimbolton, well away from London; her charge, Mary, to whom she had been *'a second mother'* had been taken from her and sent, aged seventeen, to live amongst her enemies; and the King was attacking the Church which had seemed eternal. He was also rounding on anyone who had had dealings with Elizabeth Barton, the Nun of Kent.

Barton had made a number of prophecies over the years, and, having been examined by William Warham, Archbishop of Canterbury, found to be a woman of purity. In earlier times, Henry had met the Nun himself and listened to her, but now she was beginning to criticise him and his policies. There was a hunt for all those who appeared to have given credence to her loud proclamations against Henry's second marriage.

Katharine had refused to have anything to do with Barton, and had instructed Margaret to keep the Nun well away from Mary, but it was alleged that Margaret had had the Nun's prophecies concerning the King's imminent death repeated to her. In such turbulent times, it is not surprising that Margaret, now sixty, fell ill, and lay for several months on a sickbed at Bisham. The Nun's prognostications were particularly sensitive because they touched on the succession, a matter over which Henry was increasingly touchy, especially where his blood relatives were concerned.

Margaret lay low for the next three years, but not low enough. In 1535, she became involved in a dispute with Cromwell over the appointment of one William Barlow as Prior of Bisham. Bisham Priory was the ancestral mausoleum of the Earls of Salisbury and Margaret would normally expect a say in the appointment – she had certainly complained about the previous prior, although she now lobbied to have him retained. Barlow was not favoured by Margaret as he was a strong supporter of Henry's marriage to Anne Boleyn. Not surprisingly, Barlow was appointed despite Margaret's opposition.

Chapter 8: Mother of the King's Enemy (1536 – 1538)

In 1536, the Wheel of Fortune seemed to begin to turn again in Margaret's favour. Anne Boleyn was disgraced and executed, and Henry's third wife was a strong sympathiser with his elder daughter, now degraded from 'Princess' Mary, to mere 'Lady' Mary. Margaret reappeared at Court in June 1536, but the price of Mary's rehabilitation and forgiveness was the acceptance that her parents' marriage had been invalid. She was finally forced to accept the Act of Supremacy, and swallowed the bitter pill on 22nd June 1536.

It was believed that, with this change of Queen, and the return of Mary to Court, Margaret's influence would increase, and she began to be supplicated for favours as before, but Fortune had smiled, only to dash Margaret to the ground.

Reginald Pole, her son, had been studying in Europe, at Henry's expense, for many years. He was extremely well-thought of in Church circles, as a scholar, a man of sober life, and, of course, as a cousin of the King of England. He was a very influential figure in Rome and having studied the matter of Henry and Katharine's marriage, appeared, initially, to be in favour of annulment. He did not make any definitive statements in the early 1530s, despite being offered the Archbishopric of York, but then, in October 1535, he had written to Cromwell asking the latter:

' *to assure His Highness of my readiness to do him service at all times'.*

Henry obviously took this as a sign that Reginald was about to declare in his favour, so the arrival of a second, open letter, entitled *De Unitate*, in June 1536, was the Tudor equivalent of a bombshell. Reginald referred to Henry as:

'a robber, murderer and greater enemy to Christianity than the Turk.'

Not only that, he actively called upon Charles V and François I to invade the kingdom and depose Henry.

The first news Margaret had of this incendiary missive was when she was summoned to the King's presence and he told her in person of the outrageous, treasonable, ungrateful, perverse, ignorant etc etc behaviour of her son. There is no record, of course, of the actual conversation, but we can imagine Henry's fury. He was beside himself with rage - and the wrath of a Prince is death.

Margaret immediately consulted with her eldest son, Henry, Lord Montague, as to the best course of action for the family to take. Margaret and Montague were no doubt genuinely horrified that Reginald had uttered such appalling insults against the King. Even if, in their hearts, they opposed the divorce, and perhaps, the Royal Supremacy (although there is no indication they had made any difficulties in the matter on religious grounds), the King was still an almost sacred being. Insulting him was a shocking act of disobedience.

Montague and Margaret were both well aware that treason was a miasma that could envelope a whole family. They decided to inform all of their servants that Reginald was a traitor, and that he was to be reported to the authorities if he arrived in England. Margaret *'took her son for a traitor and for no son, and that she would never take him otherwise.'*

The King wanted more, and so Margaret wrote directly to Reginald, saying she could not bear the King's wrath. He should

'...take another way and serve our master as thy bounden duty is to do unless thou wilt be the confusion of thy mother'.

If he did not remember what was due to the King he could *'trust never in (her).'*

Henry continued to fume, and sent for Montague whom he harangued with quotes from Reginald's letter. Montague wrote to Reginald in anger and frustration, telling him not to visit the Pope, as he had heard Reginald planned, and pointing out that *'Learning you may well have but doubtless no prudence nor pity.'* If Reginald were to continue in his foolish course, Montague would disown him.

Margaret now retired from Court. Although Mary had been returned to the King's good graces, and had been allowed to select members of her new household, there was no place for Margaret in it. Having capitulated and accepted the annulment, Mary had more sense than to provoke her father again. Margaret and her god-daughter exchanged gifts at New

Year (although, significantly, there were no gifts from the King) but did not meet again.

The Countess was in her sixties, and perhaps was content with a more retired life although she still took a very active part in managing her estates, and was kept occupied with the business of educating her grand-daughters and training them up to be great ladies in their turn.

Sadly, this quiet retirement did not last long.

Chapter 9: The Wrath of a Prince (1538 – 1541)

Throughout the early 1530s, Margaret's sons (other than Reginald) had supported Henry VIII's government, accepting the Act of Supremacy, and the Act of Succession.

Even after the nightmare of Reginald's 1536 letter, Montague was retained at Henry's side and when, in October 1536, the major uprising, known as the Pilgrimage of Grace, broke out, Montague and Geoffrey acted in accordance with their duty, bringing 200 men and 20 respectively to the King's forces.

Montague was in high enough favour to attend the Earl of Sussex at the christening of Prince Edward at Hampton Court in 1537 and he also supported Lady Mary in her role as Chief Mourner at the funeral of Jane Seymour.

In early 1537, the immediate danger of rebellion was averted but the political mood remained tense and there were still worries over the succession, and very real concern about a foreign invasion. It was during this period that Henry began strengthening England's coastal defences with structures such as Deal, Dover and Portchester Castles.

By 1538, Geoffrey was blotting the family copy book almost as badly as Reginald, although in Geoffrey's case it was not principle that he was defending. Geoffrey was notoriously feckless, quarrelsome and debt-ridden, although these faults were, for many, redeemed by his charm. Nevertheless, a mounting series of ill-judged incidents led to him being refused entrance to Court on the day of Prince Edward's christening.

Meanwhile, Henry VIII was still determined to have revenge on Reginald, whom the Pope had provokingly named as a Cardinal in 1537, despite Reginald not actually being a priest, and assassins were sent to seek Reginald out in Europe, although without success. In fairness to Henry, it should be noted that he was not a great advocate of secret assassination.

The fear of foreign invasion was given further impetus by the signing of the Treaty of Nice in July 1538 between Francois I of France and Emperor Charles V. Reginald Pole was involved in the negotiations, and the Treaty was seen, in part, as preparation for an invasion of England.

Sometime in June 1538, one Gervase Tyndall, an informer reporting to Thomas Cromwell, was staying, whether by accident or design is not certain, in an infirmary maintained by Margaret. The surgeon in charge, a man named Richard Ayer, passed away the hours with his inmate gossiping about his employer, Lady Salisbury and her family.

What he had to say made Tyndall's ears prick up, and he was soon reporting back to Cromwell that the Pole brothers in England were communicating with their brother, Reginald. It also came to light that Lady Salisbury and her Council had forbidden the reading of the Bible in English, in contravention of the new law.

Despite Montague's best efforts to conform, and Margaret's quiet retirement, events were closing in on the family. On 29th August 1538, Geoffrey was arrested and taken to the Tower of London, where he languished for two months before being questioned: presumably the delay was planned to give him plenty of time to reflect on the wisdom of pleasing the King with his answers to his interrogators.

He was joined in early November by Montague and the Marquess of Exeter, Henry's first cousin, as well as various others. All were charged with treason.

On 12th November, the Earl of Southampton and the Bishop of Ely arrived at Margaret's home at Warblington Castle. She was questioned, then taken to confinement at Cowdray Castle, Southampton's seat.

The evidence against Montague and the others relates to letters and other communication between Geoffrey and Montague at home, and Reginald, still blasting the King from the safety of Europe. The content of the letters was the usual litany of complaints about the world being turned upside down, and warnings that Reginald was under threat from assassins. Geoffrey, being loose-tongued, had talked foolishly, and there was a fair case against him.

Unfortunately, whilst trying to limit the damage he had done, Geoffrey mentioned other names, including Montague's, and the more he tried to say to show they were innocent, the worse it sounded. Terrified (as would we all be) by the threat of torture and the fear that he would implicate his family, Geoffrey tried to commit suicide. Prevented, he was interrogated again.

Meanwhile, Margaret was being questioned at length at Cowdray. In the answers, copied at the time and signed in her own hand, she disclaimed the slightest involvement of either herself or Montague with any sort of treason.

'..If ever it be found and proved in her, that she is culpable in any of those things, that she hath denied, that she is content to be blamed in the rest of all the articles laid against her.'

She denied absolutely that she had received any letters from Reginald (there is one he apparently wrote to her, but it was sent to Montague, so she may well not have received it.) She also denied that she had heard of the destruction of other letters, or that she had heard her sons make any comments about the world being turned upside down. Nor had she ever heard Geoffrey or Montague say that they wanted to join Reginald, although she admitted she knew Reginald had escaped the assassins, at which *'for motherly pietie...she [rejoiced].'*

Her interrogators marvelled at her tenacity and probably believed her. The Earl of Southampton wrote to Cromwell:

'..[either] her sons have not made her privy ne participant of the bottom and pit [of] their stomachs, or else is she the [most] arrant traitoress that ever [lived].'

He also described her as *'rather a strong and constant man, than a woman'*. A kind of compliment, to Tudor minds!

Despite the best efforts of Geoffrey and Margaret to show that Montague was in no way involved in treason, on 2nd December 1538 he was tried and convicted and on the 9th he was beheaded on Tower Hill. On 2nd January 1539, Geoffrey was excused the death penalty, but was to remain in the Tower. He again attempted suicide.

The question then became, what to do with Margaret? There was no evidence against her, but as a powerful magnate she controlled huge swathes of land on the south coast. With the very real fears of an invasion by France or the Empire, it would have been foolhardy to leave her free.

An Act of Attainder was passed against her in May 1539, confiscating her Earldom and demoting her once again to Lady Margaret Pole. Southampton and his wife were fed up with holding her in their home at Cowdray. Margaret clearly knew how to make herself unpleasant and difficult and Lady Southampton refused to be left alone with her *'in nowise would she tarry behind me, the said Lady being in my house.'*

By 20th November 1540 Margaret had been dispatched to the Tower, and she and Montague's young son were not included in the general pardon issued in 1540. Exeter's wife (who had more involvement in the matter than Margaret) had been pardoned and given an income, so it is not unreasonable to assume that part of the reason for Margaret's continued incarceration was personal dislike of Margaret, and the desire for revenge on Reginald Pole, by Henry.

Nevertheless, whilst in the Tower, Henry paid reasonable sums for Margaret's maintenance, and the wages of her waiting woman. Now elderly, Margaret was suffering from the cold and asked for warmer clothes. In March 1541, perhaps beginning to relent, the King ordered furred gowns and warm footwear for her – maybe Fortune's Wheel was moving in the right direction at last?

But no, Margaret's star was about to be extinguished once and for all. Whilst the warm clothes were being ordered, a new investigation into correspondence between Reginald and two of the King's Ambassadors, Sir John Wallop (a relative of the Poles) and Sir Thomas Wyatt was ordered. Margaret's former steward was also questioned. Then came news of an uprising in the North.

On 27th May, 1541, Margaret was beheaded in the Tower. Few details are known, but it appears to have been a spur of the moment decision. No scaffold had been built, and a small block was improvised. Margaret was informed that she was about to die on the very morning itself. She protested that *'she found the thing very strange, not knowing of what crime she was accused, nor how she had been sentenced.'*

She must have been woken early, as at 7am she was led out onto Tower Green. As was customary, she was allowed to speak. She commended her soul to God and asked the bystanders to pray for the King, the Prince and for Princess Mary. Remembering the god-daughter who had been so dear to her, she sent her blessing, and asked Mary's in return. The guards were becoming fidgety, so she was told to '*make haste and place her neck on the block*'.

The hastiness of the execution and the absence of the usual executioner, who had been sent north to deal with the rumoured uprising, meant that Margaret was left to suffer at the hands of '*a wretched and blundering youth...who...hacked her head and shoulders to pieces.*' Her butchered remains were buried in the Chapel of St Peter ad Vincula in the Tower, where they were discovered in 1876.

The reaction of Reginald to her death was to declare her a martyr who had died for her faith. This view was taken up by the Roman Catholic Church, and in 1886, Margaret was beatified, consequently being known in the Roman Catholic Calendar as the Blessed Margaret Pole, who had not hesitated to '*lay down [her] life by the shedding of [her] blood ...for the truth of the orthodox Faith*'.

This was her son's belief at the time, but, whilst one hesitates to question the received opinion of Margaret as dying for her faith, there is no evidence at all that she ever seriously challenged Henry VIII's religious changes. Unlike More or Fisher, she did not refuse to conform, and, although she may have made her private distaste more obvious than was wise, there was no occasion when she was faced with a stark choice of conformity or death.

The injustice of her death lies in the very fact that she was obviously innocent of all of the charges of treason that ensnared her sons.

Aspects of Lady Margaret Pole's Life

Chapter 10: Margaret Pole: Feudal Magnate

In 1512, Margaret petitioned for the return of the Salisbury inheritance. The Earldom of Salisbury had first been granted to William de Montacute (the name is variously rendered as Montacute, Montague and Montagu), a close friend of Edward III, on 16th March 1337

It then descended over the next hundred years through sons and brothers until, in 1428, it was vested in Alice Montacute. Alice was married to Richard Neville, son of Ralph Neville, Earl of Westmorland and Lady Joan Beaufort. Neville, who had an older half-brother who preceded him in the Westmorland inheritance, was recognised as Earl of Salisbury in his wife's right.

The lands of the Earldom were vast, concentrated mainly in the counties of Hampshire and Wiltshire, although the family mausoleum was at Bisham Priory in Buckinghamshire. Countess Alice had ten children, who married into the various noble families of the kingdom, some becoming supporters of York, and others of Lancaster.

Alice's own husband, and her eldest son, another Richard Neville (known as Earl of Warwick in the right of his wife, Anne Beauchamp), were initially York's strongest supporters. Her husband was killed with his brother-in-law, Richard, Duke of York, at the Battle of Wakefield on 30th December 1460, and Anne died within two years.

However, by 1462, the House of York had been victorious, and Anne's son succeeded to her inheritance, although he continued to be known as

Earl of Warwick – and, in later years as Warwick the Kingmaker. For, in 1470, Warwick reconciled with Lancaster, and replaced Edward IV of York with Henry VI. In due course, Edward IV was triumphant, and Warwick was killed at the Battle of Barnet in 1471.

Warwick's wife, Countess Anne was still alive, and, in strict law, should have retained her Earldom, but Warwick's daughters (the couple had no sons) were married to King Edward's brothers, George, Duke of Clarence, and Richard, Duke of Gloucester and so all her lands were distributed between the brothers and their wives, as well as the lands of the Salisbury Earldom. Poor Countess Anne was to be treated as though she were 'naturally dead', according to the grants to Clarence and Gloucester.

The older sister, Isabel Neville, Duchess of Clarence, had two children, Edward, who was named as Earl of Warwick, and granted his mother's share of the Warwick lands on his birth, and Margaret. On Clarence's execution for treason, young Warwick, aged only five, inherited his mother's share of the Salisbury lands. His cousin, Edward of Middleham, son of Anne Neville, Duchess of Gloucester, stood to inherit the remainder, on Anne's death. Sadly, Edward of Middleham, by then styled Prince of Wales, as the son of Richard III, died young, followed, shortly thereafter by his mother. All of the Salisbury and Warwick lands therefore vested in Edward, Earl of Warwick, whose natural heir, until he married, was his sister Margaret.

There was no chance of the Earl of Warwick marrying. Kept under close watch first by his uncle Richard III, then by the new king, Henry VII, by 1487 he was in the Tower of London, never to emerge.

Henry VII, who liked to have a legal cloak to cover his financial exactions, suddenly remembered the plight of poor Countess Anne, defrauded twenty years before by her sons-in-law, and restored the

Warwick lands to her. There was a catch – she was to disinherit her grandson, and will the lands to Henry himself.

Thus, when Warwick was executed, allegedly for attempting to escape from the Tower, in 1499, he had rights only to the Salisbury earldom, which rights devolved to his sister, Margaret, now married to Sir Richard Pole.

Lady Margaret and Sir Richard did not breathe a word about the loss of Margaret's inheritance whilst Henry VII was alive, but in 1512, with Henry VIII on the throne, and Margaret's friend, Katharine of Aragon as Queen, Margaret (now widowed) made a claim to have the Earldom of Salisbury restored to her.

She carefully worded her petition so that no word of blame fell on Henry VII, and did not try to unpick the will of Countess Anne of Warwick. Her request was to be restored to '*the estate, name, degree, style and title of Countess of Salisbury*' for herself and her heirs. The petition was granted, and was to take place on Ladyday 1513, from which point Margaret would take the income – although, in the event, it was 1st January 1514 before she took possession.

Excluded from the restoration were any lands the King could claim as the heir of Margaret Beaufort, or any rights he might have to the lands other than their confiscation from Margaret's brother. These were important reservations, and led to some trouble for Margaret later when she persisted in a suit for certain manors that the King claimed (with some justification) belonged to him.

As was usual when an heir took possession, Margaret had to pay an entry fine – in this case, 5,000 marks, (£3,333). This equated to about eighteen months income. The first instalment of 1,000 marks was receipted by Cardinal Wolsey in May 1513, and Margaret and her eldest son, referred to from that point as Henry, Lord Montague, gave a bond for payment of the remainder.

The Salisbury lands were vast, extending into seventeen counties of England, from Lincolnshire to the Isle of Wight, and even Calais. The main concentration of lands was in Devon, Somerset, Hampshire and Buckinghamshire, with major baronial seats at Clavering in Essex and Bisham in Buckinghamshire, as well as the grand palace of Le Herber in London which, in 1458 could accommodate the Earl and 500 men.

Le Herber, later remodelled and owned by Sir Francis Drake, is now under Cannon Street Station. Margaret's annual income by the late 1530s was some £2,300, rather more than the Dukes of Norfolk and Suffolk.

The first of her houses that Margaret spent time and money renovating was Bisham, in Buckinghamshire. It was a large property, with a mediaeval great hall, and several other chambers. It was also conveniently close to her married home of Bockmer, which was now passed to her son Montague. Bisham's Priory, which had been founded by William Montacute, 1st Earl of Salisbury, was the resting place of Warwick the Kingmaker, Margaret's brother, Edward, Earl of Warwick, and her son, Sir Arthur Pole, after his death in the late 1520s. On Margaret's death, Henry reserved Bisham for himself.

Despite Bisham being the resting place of many of the Salisbury Earls, Margaret commissioned one of the most fabulous chantry chapels in England, at Christchurch Priory, where she intended to rest for ever by the side of her husband, Sir Richard. The fan vaulted ceilings are of the most prestigious Caen stone, and the Countess' arms were originally carved into the ceiling bosses, but were defaced by the King's Commissioners in 1539, when the Priory was dissolved.

Clavering was a castle, surrounded by a moat, and the chapel there was the focus of work in 1523, with new wall paintings of saints commissioned. At Le Herber, too, Margaret's chapel was not neglected – a new tabernacle (a kind of enclosure for a statue) was commissioned for an image of the Virgin.

Margaret was not content, however, with these three grand homes and constructed a new castle at Warblington in Hampshire, about a mile inland of the coast. The castle was constructed in the newly fashionable (and very expensive) brick. It was also given a traditional air with a gatehouse, complete with arrow-slits and a moat.

Inside, there were multifarious chambers, including a great chamber, a dining chamber, parlours and a long gallery. It also had a chapel and some six or so acres of gardens and pleasure grounds.

Every element of furnishing, both hard and soft, proclaimed Margaret's rank – her arms were engraved on her silver, painted on her windows, embroidered on her hangings and even bedecked her horses' harness. She did not forget her husband, although he had died long before she came into her inheritance – some of her silver included his arms impaled with hers.

Margaret's clothes, too, proclaimed her rank – black velvet and satin, ermine and sable, tawny damask and embroidered gowns were all in her wardrobe.

Margaret kept an enormous household, in the great feudal tradition. There were nineteen chambers for her servants at Warblington – and, since lower servants slept in heaps on the floor, these must have been for the higher-ranking members of the household. The bill for wages was over £700 – which, when you realise that the total landed income she and Sir Richard Pole had enjoyed from his five manors was £170 gives an idea of the scale of the household.

In total, there were seventy-three indoor servants at Warblington, presided over by the Steward of her Household. Under the Steward were the Comptroller (accountant), the Marshal and Usher of the Hall (who seated everyone according to rank, and ensured everyone behaved in a seemly fashion – brawling was a not uncommon occurrence!)

Guests were waited on by six gentleman waiters – these would have been the sons of gentlemen, sent to her household to learn to be mannerly and to understand how things were done in a great house. She was also attended by five ladies who were her daily companions. Lady attendant to a Countess was a much coveted role – it was seen as a sort of finishing school and lesser ranking members of the nobility would have petitioned for a place for their daughters.

Central to the role of the feudal magnate was the concept of "*good lordship*". This was a system in which you promoted the virtues of your friends, relatives and dependents to other lords and accepted their protégées into your household, in the hope of spreading your influence, and, in due course, receiving some sort of reward. To the modern mind, it seems almost corrupt – the giving of a job because your mother's cousin's son's brother-in-law's friend has asked for it, but that was the way it worked. You showed your influence by arranging jobs for people, then, they would owe you a favour.

A vast estate of this sort was managed by a Council, which would have acted on her behalf in the day to day running of the estates, and there are receipts for painting '*my lady's council's*' chamber at Clavering. The members of the Council were drawn from across her lands, and would have moved around, sometimes with Margaret, sometimes separately. It was particularly important for Margaret to have a Council she could trust, as she had court duties to perform for Queen Katharine, and also as Lady Governess to Princess Mary – in the years 1525-1533 she was attached to Mary's household and would not have been able to attend to all her business herself.

Margaret's paramount duty was to ensure that her wealth and status could be passed on to her children – for her eldest son, Henry, Lord Montague, that was no problem, but the others had to be considered, too. It was not, however, considered at all a good idea to sell lands for younger sons – no, they had to be found heiresses of their own. Her son Reginald was a scholar, and although he was not ordained as a priest during Margaret's lifetime, there does not seem to have been any thought of him marrying. He was well provided for, in that the King himself was paying for his education and maintenance abroad. Henry was a very generous patron of scholars.

The second son, Arthur, was found a young widow of around 17, when he was about 20. Jane Lewknor was the only daughter of Sir Roger Lewknor, by his first wife. As both he and his second wife were approaching sixty it seemed likely that Jane would inherit his entire fortune, which included the castle of Bodiam. Margaret's younger son was also found an heiress, Constance Pakenham, although she had to share her inheritance with her sister. Just in case Montague didn't have enough with Salisbury lands, he was married to Jane Nevill, daughter of Lord Bergavenny, another gentleman of advanced age and no other children.

The most splendid match of all, however, was reserved for Ursula, Margaret's only daughter. She was married in around 1520 to Lord Henry Stafford, oldest son of Edward Stafford, 3rd Duke of Buckingham, the richest, highest ranking man in the land, after the King. The 124 manors and 12 castles (plus a couple of hundred other properties) that Buckingham owned, dwarfed Margaret's Earldom.

Unfortunately, although all of these marriages seem to have been successful on a personal level (even if Arthur was often at logger-heads with his father-in-law) not one of them turned out to be the financial success Margaret had hoped for – and paid for, in complex negotiations that are the Tudor equivalent of a merger and acquisition strategy.

Buckingham was almost as royal as the King, and obviously thought he was actually more royal. He lost his head, and all his lands in 1521, leaving Ursula married to a man who never ranked higher than baron, although some of the poorer lands were restored in the 1550s. Montague's father-in-law married again and produced a son and several more daughters, thus disinheriting Jane Nevill completely. Arthur's widow remarried (despite Margaret and Montague trying to force her into a convent in disgraceful fashion) and his children had to share their inheritance with a number of half-siblings. Finally, Geoffrey's relationship with his father-in-law was not good, and Pakenham favoured his other daughter's husband in his will.

It is apparent that Margaret saw herself as the equal of any Earl of Salisbury before her, and of any noble in the kingdom. The confiscation of her earldom in 1540 must have been the most crushing blow, after the loss of her husband and sons, which she could have suffered. She had brought the family to the pinnacle of power, and had it all taken away. The Wheel of Fortune had turned.

Chapter 11: Following the Footsteps of Margaret Pole

Margaret's birthplace, the castle of Farleigh, near Farleigh Hungerford, on the border between Wiltshire and Somerset is now a ruin, in the care of English Heritage. At the time of her birth it was a splendid, modern residence, that had been seized from the Lancastrian Hungerford family and granted to Edward IV's brother, Richard, Duke of

Gloucester. Why Margaret was born there, rather than in one of her parents' many houses, is unknown.

Margaret's home until she was around five years old was probably the enormous Warwick Castle – still one of the most impressive castles in all of England. It had been part of the inheritance of her mother, Isabel Neville, daughter of the Earl of Warwick and was the main seat of her parents, the Duke and Duchess of Clarence. Warwick Castle was the birthplace of Margaret's brother, Edward, and was also the place where her mother, Duchess Isabel, died in late 1477, when Margaret was only four.

It is highly unlikely that she attended the burial of her mother, whose body was taken to Tewkesbury Abbey, where it had not lain long before it was joined by that of Margaret's father, George, Duke of Clarence, executed in the Tower of London in 1478.

Margaret's whereabouts for the next seven years is uncertain, although it is likely that she was a member of the Court, and thus would have moved between the Palaces of Westminster and perhaps Sheen and Eltham.

By 1485, she, together with her brother and her cousins, the sisters of the deposed Edward V, were in Sheriff Hutton Castle, another of the great Neville Castles that had been part of the Warwick patrimony, but granted in this instance to Margaret's aunt Anne, and her husband, the Duke of Gloucester who was now Richard III. Sheriff Hutton, today a ruin, is cared for by English Heritage – but it is still possible to get a sense of its huge scale and grandeur.

So far as is known, this was the only time Margaret spent in the north of England. In 1485, she returned to London, and was put into the care of Lady Margaret Beaufort, but where exactly they lived is unknown. Soon, she was in attendance at Court, and was present at the christening, in Winchester Cathedral, of Prince Arthur, and at Westminster Abbey for the coronation of Elizabeth of York in 1487.

Following her marriage, probably in 1487, Margaret, now Lady Margaret Pole, moved to her new husband, Sir Richard Pole's home at Bockmer, in Buckinghamshire, of which there is now no trace.

In the late 1490s Sir Richard and Lady Margaret were given the use of the King's castle at Stourton in Staffordshire, to enable Sir Richard to perform his duties in the Welsh Marches. It is here that Margaret's most famous son, Reginald, Cardinal Pole was born in 1500. Stourton, which had at one time been owned by Margaret's father, dated from the 1100s. Much changed over the intervening centuries and it is now in private hands.

Sir Richard and Lady Margaret then moved to the impressive Ludlow Castle, where Sir Richard acted as Lord Chamberlain to Arthur, Prince of Wales, and Margaret was almost certainly there as well, as Lady-in-Waiting to Arthur's wife Katharine of Aragon. To mark the marriage of Arthur and Katharine, Sir Richard commissioned a carved screen for Aberconwy Abbey, on the north coast of Wales.

After the Prince's death in 1502, and burial at Worcester Cathedral, which Margaret may have attended, she probably spent most of her time between Stourton and Bockmer, until Sir Richard's death in 1504. In later years, Margaret built a tomb for herself and Sir Richard at Christchurch Priory, in what must be one of the most stunning examples of late mediaeval English gothic. It was finished in 1529, but the couple were never interred there.

Left as a widow with four children and a very small income, Margaret retired to Bockmer, but the management of the estate was in the King's hands, as the heir, her son Henry Pole, was a minor.

In 1509, Margaret returned to Court as one of the chief ladies of the court of the new King Henry VIII and his wife, her old friend, Katharine of Aragon. Margaret was in attendance on the Queen, and would have divided her time between the new palace at Richmond, and the King and Queen's favourite haunt, the Palace of Placentia, at Greenwich.

In 1512, Margaret was restored to the Earldom of Salisbury, held by her great-grandmother. It was a fabulously rich Earldom, and as Countess in her own right, she was now possessed of several castles and literally dozens of manor houses. Her four main residences were Le Herber, in London (only the very wealthiest nobles had London houses); Clavering, in Essex; Bisham in Buckinghamshire, close to Bisham Priory, the mausoleum of the Montacute Earls of Salisbury, and the new castle she built for herself at Warblington in Hampshire.

Bisham Abbey is now a sports centre, and nothing remains of Clavering or Le Herber (buried under Cannon St station). A single Tudor tower remains at Warblington, but it is on private ground.

In the mid-1520s, Lady Margaret returned to the Welsh Marches, now as Lady Governess to a new heir to the throne, Henry and Katharine's daughter, Mary. Mary was not officially invested as Princess of Wales, but she went to Ludlow Castle, and the surrounding royal residences of Tickenhill and Hartlebury Castle, as well as the mighty Thornbury, confiscated from the Duke of Buckingham in 1521.

Both Tickenhill and Hartlebury were remodelled in the eighteenth century. Tickenhill is in private hands, but Hartlebury is open to the public. Thornbury can also be visited, as it is a luxury hotel!

Following the marriage of Henry VIII to Anne Boleyn, Princess Mary's household was dissolved and Lady Salisbury retired to her estates, spending most of her time at Warblington.

She was at Warblington in November 1538 when the King's men came to question her about alleged treasonable activities. She was taken under guard to Cowdray Castle, home of the Earl of Southampton, where she was held until December of 1539 when she was removed to the Tower of London. The Tower was to be her last resting place – she was clumsily executed in 1541, and her mangled corpse was hastily buried in the Chapel of St Peter ad Vincula, within the Tower walls.

Key to Map

1. Farleigh Castle, Somerset
2. Tewkesbury Abbey
3. Warwick Castle
4. Tower of London
5. Sheriff Hutton, Yorkshire
6. Westminster Abbey
7. Stourton Castle, Stourbridge, Staffordshire
8. Christchurch Priory
9. Bockmer House, Buckinghamshire
10. Sheen Palace
11. Ludlow Castle
12. Aberconwy Church
13. Bisham Priory
14. Palace of Placentia, Greenwich
15. Le Herber
16. Clavering Castle, Essex
17. Warblington Castle
18. Thornbury Castle
19. Tickenhill Manor
20. Hartlebury Castle, Worcestershire
21. Cowdray Castle, Sussex

Chapter 12: Margaret Pole: Two Book Reviews

There is only one modern biography of Margaret, Countess of Salisbury that we have come across. Her life is mentioned in a plethora of works on the Wars of the Roses, the life of Mary I, and, in passing, in the biographies of her son, Reginald. We have reviewed two of the most important works here.

Margaret Pole, Countess of Salisbury (1473 – 1541)

Author: Hazel Pierce

Publisher: University of Wales Press (1 February 2009)

In a nutshell: This is an excellent, well-researched, academic study of the life of Margaret, Countess of Salisbury. Particularly suitable for readers who have good knowledge of the wider events of the period and want detailed information about Margaret.

Pierce's work concentrates on putting Margaret into the context of her time, first in her traditional role of daughter, niece and wife, but then in the very unusual context of Margaret as a great landowner, wielding the level of power and patronage normally reserved for men.

The author's great skill is in exploring the contemporary records to create a portrait of Margaret that shows her as an essentially mediaeval figure – believing, first in her duty to God, then to the King, but, only just behind her allegiance to the monarch, her duty to promote her family's wealth and position to the utmost extent of her ability.

Pierce has delved extensively into Margaret's management of her estates, and demonstrates that, whilst her situation as a Countess in her own right was unusual, Margaret had no hesitation in behaving in exactly the same way as her male counterparts - often ruthless and even unscrupulous in her determination to wring the last drop from every bargain. The treatment of her widowed daughter-in-law is shown to be particularly unsavoury - Jane Lewknor was strong armed by Margaret and Margaret's eldest son, Lord Montague, into taking a vow of chastity within weeks of her husband, Arthur Pole's death, to protect the inheritance of Arthur's children.

Margaret's determination is not specifically used to advance any issues of gender politics, however it is apparent that, regardless of any convention of the time about the weakness and inferiority of women, Margaret was not going to tolerate a position as a mild and dutiful ornament. She knew her rights, and she demanded them, whilst still conforming to a mediaeval pattern of feminine chastity and conventional piety.

The relationship between Margaret and her god-daughter, Princess Mary, and her efforts to shield Mary from the worst effects of Henry VIII's annulment suit are given a very human touch, without the author making any claims that can't be substantiated by records.

Margaret's terrible death at the hands of an unskilled headsman have added to the picture of her as a martyr for her faith, but Pierce's forensic analysis of the Exeter conspiracy shows quite clearly that Margaret was innocent of any plot (no matter how vague or insubstantial it might have been) to overthrow Henry and the Royal Supremacy. Whilst it may not quite accord with the picture of her as halfway to sainthood (Margaret was beatified by the Roman Catholic Church in 1886) it makes the injustice of her execution even more outrageous.

I would love to meet the Margaret that Hazel Pierce has revealed – but I wouldn't want to try to cheat her of her rights!

*

The Hollow Crown

Author: Dan Jones

Publisher: Faber & Faber (2nd September 2014)

In a nutshell: A panoramic sweep through English History from the marriage of Henry V in 1420, to the death of Margaret Plantagenet, Countess of Salisbury in 1541. A really thorough analysis, for experts and newcomers alike – fast-moving but with enormous amounts of detail packed into every paragraph.

It is generally not hard to tell whether a writer's sympathies lie with Lancaster or York, but in the case of 'The Hollow Crown', Jones is even-handed and judicious throughout. His devastating critique of Henry VI as entirely unfit for the inheritance left him by that Plantagenet hero, Henry V, is matched by his incisive portrait of Richard, Duke of York, as self-important, partisan and as lacking in political finesse as Queen Marguerite of Anjou.

The political theory that underlies the whole work is that, in the late middle ages, having a king of legitimate royal descent was not enough for the realm to function effectively. If the character of the man wearing the Crown were not sufficiently robust, and he failed to wield his power effectively, there was no way of filling the vacuum.

During the minority of Henry VI, his uncles and the other magnates held the realm together reasonably successfully, but there was no prescription for the ills that followed from an adult king who could not step up his responsibilities. Yet, the lords were hamstrung in reacting to the situation. Henry was not a tyrant – rather he was a gentle and kindly man, so there was no excuse for his overthrow. Attempts by others to manage the kingdom on Henry's behalf, were resented and feared by both the nobles excluded from the King's inner circle, and the public at large. Jones rehabilitates William de la Pole, Earl of Suffolk, who is often vilified, but, initially, at least, tried to keep Henry's rule on track.

As royal authority disintegrated in the 1440s and 1450s, there was growing discontent, and personal feuds between members of the nobility began to get out of hand – a situation not helped by Henry's wife, Marguerite of Anjou.   It is hard not to admire some aspects of Marguerite's character as Jones presents her – she was phenomenally brave, determined and resolute in her attempts to protect the throne for her husband and son, but she was violently partisan, and, rather than rising above Court rivalries, she made the situation far worse.

Jones moves smoothly through the numerous battles that took place up and down the land, and keeps the reader on top of the dizzying changes of loyalties that characterised the period as the Crown became a plaything of the man with the biggest army.   It is with a sense of relief, that must echo that of the population of 1471, that we read of the triumph of Edward IV at Tewkesbury, bringing a King to the throne who had something of the skill, tenacity and strategic brilliance of Henry V: a man whom the vast majority of Lancastrians were willing to accept as King, with Edward of Lancaster dead.   The murder of Henry VI was skated over by most people as a little local difficulty.

But knocking an old and incompetent man on the head was one thing – usurping the throne of a twelve year old boy was quite another.   Jones shows clearly how the usurpation of Richard III undermined all of the good work done by Edward IV.   Richard may have had good instincts in how he wanted to rule, but nothing could undo the damage of his grab for the throne.   Jones is no revisionist – it is perfectly plain to him that Richard had his nephews murdered.   This one act, against all odds, united the remnants of Lancaster with the supporters of Edward IV, and brought the obscure Henry Tudor, Earl of Richmond, to the throne.

Unlike most historians, Jones does not bring the Wars to a close in 1485, or 1487 with Henry VII's victory at Stoke. He goes on to show how the lingering suspicion, the fear that any plausible rogue with an army could emulate the success of Henry in overthrowing an anointed monarch, slowly poisoned Henry's reign and led to the imprisonment and execution of almost anyone with a vague claim to the throne.

A new era appeared to dawn in 1509, with the accession of Henry VIII, heir to both Lancaster and York, but still the old fears ran deep. After an early attempt to bring the extended royal family together to turn the nobility's minds towards that perennial delight, war with France, dissensions from Henry's policies began to emerge. Nevertheless, Jones contends, the main focus was no longer the old one of York v. Lancaster, but, increasingly, families were divided between Catholic and Protestant. The final purge of possible claimants to the throne in 1538 – 41 when Montague, Exeter and the aged Countess of Salisbury were executed, was the last effusion of Plantagenet blood.

'*The Hollow Crown*' demands concentration – a huge amount of ground is covered – but it is well worth it. I can promise you will not be bored for a moment!

Bibliography

Calendar of State Papers Simancas, British History Online (HMSO, 1892) Hume, Martin A S, ed.,

Calendar of State Papers: Venice <http://www.british-history.ac.uk/cal-state-papers/venice/vol2/vii-lxi> [accessed 7 October 2015]

Cavendish, George, *Life of Cardinal Wolsey* (Forgotten Books 2009)

Letters and Papers, Foreign and Domestic, of the Reign of Henry VIII: Preserved in the Public Record Office, the British Museum, and Elsewhere in England (United Kingdom: British History Online, 2014) https://www.british-history.ac.uk/letters-papers-hen8/ Brewer, John Sherren, and James Gairdner,

De Lisle, Leanda, *Tudor: The Family Story* (United Kingdom: Chatto & Windus, 2013)

Dodds, M. H. and Dodds, R. (1971) *The Pilgrimage of Grace, 1536-1537 and the Exeter Conspiracy, 1538*. London: Frank Cass Publishers.

Ellis, Henry, *Original Letters, Illustrative of English History: Including Numerous Royal Letters: From Autographs in the British Museum, the State Paper Office, and One or Two Other Collections.*, 1st edn (New York: Printed for Harding, Triphook, & Lepard, 1824)

Fletcher, A. and Vernon, L. (1973) *Tudor Rebellions (Seminar Studies in History)*. 2nd edn. Harlow: Longman.

Fraser, Antonia, *The Six Wives of Henry VIII*, First (London: Weidenfeld & Nicolson, 1992)

Hall, Edward, *Hall's Chronicle.* (S.l.: Ams Press, 1909)

Hayward, Maria, ed., *The Great Wardrobe Accounts of Henry VII and Henry VIII* (United Kingdom: London Record Society, 2012)

Holinshed, Raphael, *Holinshed's Chronicles of England, Scotland & Ireland* (United Kingdom: AMS Press, 1997)

Hutchinson, Robert, *Thomas Cromwell: The Rise and Fall of Henry VIII's Most Notorious Minister* (London: Weidenfeld & Nicolson, 2007)

Jerdan, William, ed., *Rutland Papers. Original Documents Illustrative of the Courts and Times of Henry VII. and Henry VIII. Selected from the Private Archives of His Grace the Duke of Rutland* (Leopold Classic Library, 2015)

Jones, D. (2014) *The Hollow Crown: The Wars of the Roses and the Rise of The Tudors.* 1st edn. United Kingdom: Faber & Faber Non-Fiction.

Merriman, Roger Bigelow, *Life and Letters of Thomas Cromwell: 2 Volumes* (Oxford Scholarly Classics) (Oxford: Oxford University Press, USA, 1901)

Morse H., *Select Documents Of English Constitutional History*, ed. by George Burton Adams and Morse H Stephens (United States: Kessinger Publishing, 2007)

Perry, Maria, *Sisters to the King*, 2nd edn (Andre Deutsch, 2002)

Pierce, H. (2009) *Margaret Pole, Countess of Salisbury: 1473 - 1541: loyalty, lineage and leadership.* Cardiff: University of Wales Press.

Scarisbrick, J. J., *Henry VIII (Yale English Monarchs Series)* (Yale University Press 2 April 1997)

Starkey, David, *Six Wives of Henry VIII* (London: Vintage, 2004)

Starkey, David, *The Reign of Henry VIII: Personalities and Politics* (United Kingdom: Trafalgar Square, 1991)

Strickland, A. and Strickland, E. (2011) *Lives of the Queens of England from the Norman Conquest: Volume 3 & 4*. United Kingdom: Cambridge University Press (Virtual Publishing).

Thornton, Tim, 'Henry VIII's Progress Through Yorkshire in 1541 and Its Implications for Northern Identities', *Northern History*, 46 (2009), 231–44 http://dx.doi.org/10.1179/174587009x452323

Tremlett, G. (2010) *Catherine of Aragon: Henry's Spanish Queen.* London: Faber and Faber.

Vergil, Polydore, *Anglica Historia AD 1485-1637* (Royal Historical, 1950)

Weir, Alison, *Henry VIII: King and Court* (London: Jonathan Cape, 2001)

Weir, Alison, *The Six Wives of Henry VIII*, 1st edn (London: Random House UK Distribution, 1991)

Whitelock, A. (2010) *Mary Tudor: princess, bastard, queen.* 1st edn. New York: Random House Publishing Group.

Williams, Neville, *Henry VIII and His Court.* (London: Littlehampton Book Services, 1971)

Williams, Neville, *The Cardinal and the Secretary: Thomas Wolsey and Thomas Cromwell* (United States: Macmillan, 1976)

Select Documents Of English Constitutional History, ed. by George Burton Adams and Morse H Stephens (United States: Kessinger Publishing, 2007)

www.tudortimes.co.uk

Lightning Source UK Ltd.
Milton Keynes UK
UKHW011822070419
340624UK00001B/14/P